Thoughts

by
Brian Allen Henry

CONTENTS

ACKNOWLEDGMENTS

A big thank you to my wife Shirley for her love, continued support, and ability to keep me pointed in the right direction.

Also a special thank you to Timothy A. Rhoades for his friendship and long hours dedicated to make my dream come true

Brian Allen Henry

MAGIC OF THE PEN

The poet and the reader,
They become as one,
Each line brings them closer,
Until the meaning is undone.

They may see the verse,
Clear in their mind,
But sometimes they must,
Read between the lines.

Like an open door,
For all to explore,
He opens one's mind,
Like never before.

With pen and ink,
In his special way,
He opens your eyes,
To what the words say.

FALLING STAR

Lost and forgotten dreams,
In the cracks of Broadway.
Another falls in vain,
Without the taste of fame.

Auditions in the morning,
Clearing tables every night,
Try to hang on to,
Those neon Broadway lights.

For the few that shine,
Many more are turned away,
Hoping that tomorrow might,
Be their lucky day.

For each one who leaves,
Three more come to stay,
Thinking they will see,
Their name in lights on Broadway.

WHY

Why must there be hunger in the world,
When there is no need.
Why must there be hatred in the world,
The devil plants his seed.

Why must we turn our heads,
To people in need,
Help your fellow man,
No need for greed.

Why is the question, why indeed,
Only one has the answers,
He will let us know,
When our souls are free.

SHATTERED DREAMS

Tomorrow's children,
What will they see?
A world filled with turmoil,
Hunger and disease.

Now overcome by greed,
The rich get richer,
Destroying life's seed.

A world left in disarray,
By the hands of power,
Now the children wait,
For that final hour.

When the clock strikes,
For the last time,
Nothing is left,
Only the crime.

A world left in shambles,
Because of a greedy few,
Our four fathers had a vision,
I wonder if they knew.

LOYALTY GONE

Once there was a young man,
With hopes and dreams for a simple life,
With simple things, like a family and a wife.

Loving people with whom to share,
The foundation of life,
Now left in despair.

His dreams all ended in Vietnam,
He gave a limb with regretted naught,
When he returned his deeds forgot.

Erased from sight and mind,
Their gratitude left behind,
No thanks were offered, no welcome home,
Left a cripple to fend for his own.

He sits in awe,
At what might have been,
Burdened by a world,
A world from within.

He carries on,
The best he can,
Once a Hero,
Now shunned by Uncle Sam.

COLOR OF WAR

Young soldiers gone,
Before their time,
White crosses dotting the skyline.

Rows of regrets. Why must they die?
To satisfy the greed of,
Those who run and hide?

What are they thinking,
The men who rule the land,
Why not live in peace,
And share our brothers hand

The blood of our Heroes,
Runs free in far off lands,
With no end in sight,
Why can't they understand.

There are no winners in war,
So why do we fight,
Why not live in peace,
It seems so right.

Brian Allen Henry

UNKNOWN WORLD

In the depth's,
Of the ocean,
Lie's a world unknown,
Filled with darkness,
A silent zone.

Man's exploration blinded,
To the secrets below,
Hidden down deep,
We dare not go.

It's Neptune's Kingdom,
Ruled by his hand,
An exotic world,
We'll never understand.

TIME'S VICTIM

A little town,
Silenced by the times,
Once bustling sidewalks,
With bright neon signs.

The smiling faces,
With greetings each day,
Now replaced by silence,
As their town's swept away.

Empty houses and shuttered stores,
Now they echo the past,
That once was,
Will be no more.

They closed the mill,
The heart of the town,
Nothing but memories,
And silence all around.

SELF DESTRUCT

Nowhere to turn,
Walls on all sides,
Trapped in myself,
Like an oncoming tide.

My body shakes out of control,
My needs are strong as they over take my soul.

How did I get here?
Did it start with a line?
My hunger got worse,
A day at a time.

Now I'm a slave to the demons within,
My life soon over, no way left to win.

PUPPY LOVE

There's nothing like a puppy,
To put your heart at ease.
His eyes tell your heart,
Take me home please.

You try to put it down,
But your soon give in,
When it comes to puppy love,
The puppy always win.

TRANQUIL

Open spaces no city sounds,
A man and his horse with beauty all around.

No more riding the subway,
Those days are long gone.

Traded his suit for a saddle and song,
He's where he wants to be.

At peace with himself under a western sky,
Riding along with a gleam in his eye.

Living his dream on a mountain high,
His dreams have come true as an Eagle flies by.

TIME

The sun comes up,
Another day begins,
Starting where yesterday ends.

Much will change,
Before the sun goes down,
New life on Earth others heaven bound.

It's the cycle of life,
Lived day to day,
Only death stands in the way.

Time has no end,
It just has a past,
All things move on, nothing will last

Except Time.

Brian Allen Henry

LIFE'S PASSING

When you're young,
Every days a new venture,
When you're old,
You dare not venture.

When you're young,
Life is filled with wonder,
When you're old,
You wonder how much longer.

Young or old,
One thing is for sure,
We will travel a one way road,
That leads to no more.

So my friend,
Enjoy what you can,
While you can till the end,
It's not in our hand.

LOOK WITHIN

If I could would I,
Is the intent,
If I had the magic,
Lamp to change my,
Life would I or,
Would I seek to see,
If life would be,
Better one never knows,
Like the poem ends,
It's a guessing game,
Conclusion take life as,
It comes or take risks.

Brian Allen Henry

SEASON CHANGE

Listen to a robin song,
Early on a spring morn,
The message it brings,
Winter's come and gone.

Have you watched a flower,
When nature starts its bloom,
After a spring rain,
Kissed by the Dew.

Magic is in the moment,
When springs in the air,
Brown grass turns green,
And the new leaves appear.

Awakened from their sleep,
Touched by the sun,
There's a feeling of joy,
Felt by everyone.

So take a deep breath,
And enjoy spring song,
Until the colors turn,
And winter comes along.

ALONE WITH NATURE

Adrift on the water,
Soaking up the sun,
As one with nature,
He lets his line run.

It rests out of sight,
Waiting for a strike,
Surrounded by pines,
It seems so right.

At peace with himself,
Enjoying nature's way,
Taking in the sites,
On this wondrous day.

Brian Allen Henry

CHANGING COLORS

There's nothing more beautiful,
Than an autumn day,
When the hills change their colors,
In such a special way.

Soon old man winter,
Will be coming along,
Bringing winter chill,
No more robin's song.

When the colors start to fade,
And the beauty turns to white,
Leaving autumns picture,
As just a moment in time.

SILENT MEMORIES

Laughter comes from within,
As a fire burns bright,
A family sharing love,
What a beautiful sight.

Snow falls to the ground,
Bringing a blanket of white,
To the Earth Below,
On Christmas Eve night.

Looking through a window,
Unknown to those inside,
As they exchange gifts of love,
Tears fall from my eyes.

I remember days long ago,
When I had a family to love,
Before life brought me down another road,
Like a lonely dove.

No one to share with,
No family to call my own,
Just a lost soul,
Without a loving home.

Brian Allen Henry

A SIMPLE LIFE

A bouncing ball,
Words to sing,
As in one big voice,
We all join in.

A thing of the times,
In years gone by,
When life was simple,
And we just got by.

No new age gadgets,
To pass their time,
Movies were the gathering place,
In those years gone by.

No mobile phones,
No source to text,
Just popcorn and a movie,
And time to rest.

A simple life long gone,
A way of life,
Where people were happy,
With a bouncy ball and a song.

ROUGH WATERS

It's never too late,
To turn anew,
To go back to that person,
That you once knew.

If your life is like,
A walk in the dark,
Just find life's light,
To make things right.

When you take control,
There's no despair,
Know who you are,
You'll soon be there.

The journey is yours,
And yours alone,
Just follow the light,
Until it brings you home.

Brian Allen Henry

LAND OF DREAMS

Red, White, and Blue,
Our roots run deep,
A freedom of worship,
And freedom of speech.

A place to live,
As free as the wind,
A land of plenty,
Where new life begins.

Our Lady stands proud,
She's there to catch us,
Should we fall,
Equally for one and all.

A land of promise,
Where your dreams can come true,
It's the land of plenty,
The land of the Red, White, and Blue.

MARY'S CHILD

He calls us out on Sunday morning,
He asks we sit with awhile,
He calls us out on Sunday morning,
The man we know as Mary's child.

Sometime we sit with him in silence,
Or we call his name out loud,
He's always there to guide us,
From life's darkest clouds.

Who was this man known as Jesus,
He died that we might live,
His message for all,
Life's better if you give.

Brian Allen Henry

THE MASTER'S HAND

The beauty of the
Artist brush how it,
Brings a soul to stir,
The color of the Oil's,
Make us wish we,
Could be there.

Deep in the moment,
Do we see what,
The master saw,
When he put his,
Brush to canvas,
For all to explore.

We fill his deepest,
Thoughts through a,
Self-revealing hand,
Everyone will see,
It different, no
Need to understand.

He touched our souls,
Forever with his gentle,
Stroke of art the artist,
And his image forever in our heart.

LOST SOULS

A shot rings out in the night,
Another soul has lost his life,
Was it there turf or colors,
That took him down,
Silence broken by sirens sound.

What are they thinking,
These children of the street,
Could it be their despair,
Or maybe a feeling that no one cares,
As he lays face down in the cold night air.

So they rule their turf,
It's become there way of life,
True to their colors most will die,
By the bullet or the knife.

Brian Allen Henry

GOING HOME

Pastel colors and a ceiling of blue,
My eyes were opened to something new,
The air was sweet and filled with love,
My father had called me to heaven above.

Familiar faces greet me one by one,
Now that my work on Earth is done,
Home with my father and his son.

It happened in the blink of an eye,
Not having time to say goodbye,
To my loved ones and friends,
Past life gone, new life begins.

OUT OF CONTROL

Floating through the sky,
Like a balloon on high,
It drifts to and throw
With nowhere to go.

With no direction at hand,
They just drift along,
Losing control of life,
They don't understand.

Trying to exist today,
While life's winds blow,
They end up falling,
When the breeze is slow.

The damage is done,
There's no place to hide,
Just a lost soul,
Along for the ride.

Brian Allen Henry

THE DREAM

We come from places,
All over the globe,
Young and old alike,
We walk a new road.

We seek a new life,
With freedoms at hand,
And a working appetite.

We lay our foundations,
And watch them grow with time,
The statue of liberty,
Says simply be mine.

We blend as one,
In the land of the free,
We are American,
Living our dreams with,
Equality for you and me.

THE WHISTLE

The sound of a train whistle,
Takes me away,
Like a hobo hiding,
In the shadows of a boxcar,
On a cold rainy day.

Heading for sunshine,
Somewhere down the line,
Time is his friend,
The tracks his home,
Just passing time alone.

He only wants to visit,
Never does he stay,
So next time you,
Hear the whistle sound,
Know he's on his way.

With peace in his soul,
He longs for that sound,
Of that lonely whistle,
As he makes his way,
From town to town.

Brian Allen Henry

PARADISE

A place of dreams,
We've all been there,
A place to relax,
Without a care.

A feeling so serene,
A picture in my mind,
Escape from reality,
Only for a time.

At peace with myself,
My troubles all gone,
If only a moment,
Paradise is my home.

THE OLD MAN

There was an old man,
Who lived by the tracks,
Under a tree in an old shack,
Collecting cans for daily food,
Whatever he could find,
He would make do.

People in the town say,
That he lost his wife,
In years gone by,
No one knows how or why,
He had been a doctor,
So the story goes,
Why he walked away,
No one really knows.

Outside his shack,
He sits all night,
Looking back at his past,
By the warm fire light.
Each memory brings pain,
To this lonely man,
Whose life had changed,
From a happy soul,
To a life lost in vain.

Brian Allen Henry

IN SEARCH

Alone in the world,
The streets my home,
From city to city,
I seem to roam.

Always looking for something,
I can call my own,
A soul grows tired,
When roots can't grow.

Everybody needs their space,
A place to call their own.
So my search will go on,
Until I find my home.

FACES IN THE SKY

Face's in the sky,
From the masters eye,
He moves the clouds,
On a canvas of blue,
Where imagination comes to view.

His brush never ending,
In an ever changing sky,
No two pictures the same,
As new clouds come in,
Where one ends another begins.

Brian Allen Henry

AS I WONDER

The majestic mountains,
Reach for the sky,
Like an oil painting,
In one's eyes.

I stare in wonder,
How can this be,
Such a wonderful world,
So much to see.

I takes ones breath,
To take it all in,
How did it get here,
How did it begin.

CITY BOUND

The weekend is over,
Monday rolls around,
Time to go to work,
And face the city sound.

Paperwork, paperwork,
Going through my brain,
The clock strikes five,
Time to catch my train.

I pull in the station,
Back home at last,
All the black asphalt,
Replaced by green grass.

I have some dinner,
Read the paper through,
Watch a little T.V.
I catch the local news.

I set my clock,
Soon morning will arrive,
Time to start all over,
I'm hoping to survive.

Out of the house,
I start on my way,
Heading for the city,
Another hectic day.

Brian Allen Henry

BABES AT PLAY

Through the distant trees,
I see the cubs at play,
Their mother watches over them,
If danger comes their way.

I sit in silence,
Such a wonderful sight,
The sunshine through the trees,
As I watch their playful flight.

Soon they will grow,
Have cubs of their own,
To play as they will,
This forest is their home.

LOVE LOST

Living with a memory,
Will have to do,
Our love was no more,
From out of the blue.

She said it's over,
We've drifted apart,
Time to move on,
It's time to part.

With a broken heart,
I'm left alone,
An empty house,
No longer a home.

FATHER'S WISDOM

Crawl walk and run,
This advice I give you son,
Don't be in a hurry,
To achieve your dreams,
Build a strong foundation,
Topped off with strong beams.

Then your house won't crumble,
It will be sturdy and strong,
Just like a mountain,
It will forever carry on,
Your wants and needs,
Will come to pass,
Just like the sands,
In an hour glass.

A SMILE

If eyes are the,
Window to the soul,
And your smile is,
Yours and yours alone.

It must be sincere,
And always bright,
It's your silent voice,
Your inner light.

So when your smile,
Comes from the heart,
It's a warm feeling,
Of which you're a part.

Brian Allen Henry

FRIENDSHIP

A friend is someone,
Who's always there for you,
A friends a special person,
Who knows you through and through.

There always there to help you,
No matter what the cost,
True friendship is always there,
It never will get lost.

So cherish your friends,
And let them know you care,
Because without true friends,
Life would be so bare.

CARNIVAL

The sound of a carnival,
Fills the night air,
People on rides,
Without a care.

A family affair,
Where memories are made,
A time to share laughter,
On this special day.

Weather young or old,
It's a wonderful sight,
Bringing families together,
With a feeling of delight.

FIRST CAR

My first car what a thrill,
To finally sit behind the wheel,
It's a pass to freedom,
When one comes of age,
You're the actor,
The roads your stage.

LIFE'S CYCLE

Young man where did you go,
Yesterday doesn't seem so long ago,
Day's pass with the blink of an eye,
Months, and years… how time flies.

A young man with dreams and desires,
All turned to ashes in life's fire,
I never thought I would wake one day,
To wrinkled skin and hairs of grey.

A never ending cycle life waits for no one,
It comes and goes like the setting sun.
The past is clear time doesn't lie,
What once was young, has passed you by.

Brian Allen Henry

THE MEDICINE MAN

He lives in harmony,
With the Earth's seed,
He's the medicine man,
He's a dying breed.

His healing touch,
And his spiritual soul,
Tells him all that he,
Needs to know.

He heals with wisdom,
Handed down in time,
His father's son,
The next in line.

He carries on tradition,
Knowing it must never die,
For he is the blood line,
To spirits in the sky.

THE LURE OF THE MOON

From a manned capsule,
High in the sky,
He watches the world,
As it passes by.

He goes where none,
Have gone before,
With a whole,
New world to explore.

He sends back photos,
For us to view,
Of a distant moon,
We never knew.

Brian Allen Henry

THE BOARDER

He glides down the mountain
On glistening snow,
With a board attached,
He navigates where to go.

He's one with the slopes,
An adrenaline high,
He masters the hill,
Under a clear blue sky.

When fresh snow has fallen,
He heads for the hills,
To conquer the mountains,
Oh what a thrill.

WONDERFUL WORLD

A beautiful summer day,
Filled with beauty all around,
Fields and hills full of color,
As flower's abound.

Birds sing their joyful songs,
As they build their little nest,
The little one's will be here soon,
No time for them to rest.

Reflections on the water,
Of puffy clouds on high,
While otters are at play,
By the river side.

What a wonderful feeling,
To be a part of this,
On this beautiful summer day,
One with nature in her special way.

P.O.W.

He's tortured each day,
But he won't give in,
He gives name, rank, and number,
The rest is held within.

He's caged like an animal,
Barely food to survive.
Sometimes he wonders,
What keeps him alive.

He's true to his colors,
And the land of his birth,
He will fight oppression,
With all that he's worth.

He's our countries hero,
Willing to die that we might live,
For the land of the free,
His life he would give.

RAINBOW GOLD

The arches of the rainbow,
So bright and alive,
Hanging like a picture,
So high in the sky.

From out of nowhere,
They only appear on rainy days,
With their many bright colors,
They leave you amazed.

Some say there's a leprechaun,
At the rainbows end,
Watching over his treasure,
From being stolen from him.

It might be a myth,
Or maybe it's true,
It's a tale of time,
For us all to view.

SPECIAL DAY

As she walks down the aisle,
All dressed in white,
He looks in awe, at this beautiful sight.

As she nears the alter,
His dreams coming true,
Soon they'll be one,
For their whole life through.

There special day comes,
As he takes her hand,
The vows are taken,
By this woman and man.

With love in there hearts,
They make their way,
To celebrate with friends,
On their special day.

DIFFERENT ROADS

Two brothers went walking,
Off to war one day,
One thought of blue,
While the other thought of grey.

They walked till they came,
To a fork in the road.
One kept walking,
While the other one slowed.

Brother my dear brother,
You're going the wrong way,
For that is the road,
That leads to the grey.

No my dear brother,
I have not lost my way,
For you must fight for blue,
And I must fight for grey.

They bowed their heads in sorrow,
And slowly walked away,
Knowing that one fateful day,
The blue must meet the grey.

As the guns then did fire,
On that tragic day,
The brother in blue,
Killed his brother in grey.

BE PROUD

Our flag is a symbol of unity,
It binds us as one,
It is generations of hard work,
Shared by everyone.

With its stars and stripes,
It calls out to all,
With arms wide open to catch,
Those who fall.

They call us Big Brother, Uncle Sam,
No matter the name,
We will forever stand,
As one in freedom's land.

LITTLE THINGS

As I lay in my bed,
With my window in view,
A little bird lands,
Looking through.

He moves his head,
From side to side,
And flutters his wings,
Ready to fly.

To trade him places,
What a thrill it would be,
For a paralyzed,
Cripple like me.

As he flies away,
I'm left alone,
With my hopes that,
Someday I'll be whole.

HEADS OR TAILS

Fate can be a good thing,
Your fortune is found,
Right place, wrong time,
It all turns around.

Fate can be a good thing,
Right place, the right time,
Your fortune is found,
Fate knows no bounds.

Life is but a fine line,
That is walked by all,
Fate will determine,
On which side you will fall.

SOUNDS AND SIGHTS OF NIGHT

On a quiet night,
I hear not a sound,
With the moon on high,
And stars heaven bound.

I stare into the heavens,
As a shooting star comes near,
It streaks for a moment,
Then it disappears.

Form my front porch,
The things I see,
It makes me wonder,
Are they looking at me.

GET AWAY

In my mind's eye,
I've been there before,
Escape from reality,
To an island shore.

I sit beneath a palm,
The ocean at my door,
Such a tranquil feeling,
It's mine to explore.

It's my little escape,
My place in the sun,
It's my perfect world,
That I share with no one.

PLAY BALL

Hot dogs and drinks,
Under the lights,
Supporting the home team,
Dad and me on Saturday night.

The pitcher winds up,
And lets it fly,
The batter swings,
But not in time.

The ump raises his hand,
The count is full,
As he awaits the pitch,
His bat must be true.

He sees a blur,
Through the infield lights,
He swings the bat,
The timings right.

The bat meets the ball,
It's a time of delight,
To watch the ball,
As it soars out of site.

Brian Allen Henry

TOUGH GUY

The rodeo cowboy,
A man among men,
He gives his all,
In order to win.

He's a tough hombre,
A man of true grit,
He knows not the meaning,
When it comes to quit.

On a bucking horse,
Or a wild bull's back,
He gives his soul,
As his senses react.

He ride's for a purse,
With the best score in mind,
A life of danger,
He lays it all on the line.

TIME TO PAUSE

In a world of turmoil,
Ever thing is moving so fast,
It takes over your mind,
Try to live with the future,
While dealing with the past.

With our world in change,
Stress creeps and hides within,
It breaks down our barriers,
And sickness begins inside,
A silent and deadly ride.

You see yourself change,
A day at a time,
To a stress filled world,
Like a roaring tide,
Inner peace denied.

FREEDOM'S DAY

Down main streets to joyous throngs,
The air filled with joy,
As the floats move along,
Clowns throwing candy,
To little girls and boys.

Queens on their floats,
Throw kisses all about,
With their long dresses and gowns,
Their beauty stands out.

Bringing up the rear,
Cowboys and cowgirls on horses,
Tip their hats as they pass by,
On this very festive day,
Known as the fourth of July.

SIMPLE NEEDS

No need for a mansion,
High on a hill,
No need for limousines,
And fancy frills.

Don't want the pressure,
Of wealth untold,
Life isn't all about,
Silver and Gold.

Just need a house,
With a white picket fence,
Just want a real life,
That just makes real sense.

I'd fill my dreams,
With love and joy,
A beautiful wife,
A girl and a boy.

Brian Allen Henry

THE OLD BEENIE

Let's talk about hats,
Some are big,
Others are small,
There made of cloth,
Or maybe wool.

There are hats with flaps,
There are hats with brims,
Some sit on your head,
Others buckle under your chin.

They come in many colors,
Red, white, and blue,
Some plaid, some striped,
Just to name a few.

A world without hats,
There's just no way.
Hats have been around
Forever and a day.

MY DRUMMER FRIEND

Silent drums faded smile,
A candle flickers just awhile,
The flame is gone forever still,
A soul released to greener fields.

Too soon gone to understand,
The hurting soul of the man,
Held within out of sight,
He closed his eyes and said goodbye.

A world gone wrong,
With hurt and pain,
Nothing makes sense,
To a life that's changed.

So rest my friend,
Let your hurt go free,
You had now,
Now you have Eternity.

Dedicated to Michael "Fergie" Ferguson

A friend to all, an enemy to none.
May his memory live on.

Brian Allen Henry

MY BROTHER, MY FRIEND

A big brother is,
Someone to look up to,
He's always there to,
Help me through.

Since young boys I,
Would tag along,
He watched over me,
Right or wrong.

We were best friends,
From the very start,
Even when times away
Kept us apart.

As I look back,
What a ride it's been,
I'm very lucky indeed,
To have spent it with my best friend.

NATURE'S FACE

The faces of mother nature,
Their always nearby,
She can take a clear day,
And turn it to a darkened sky.

She can bring gentle rain,
To help the crops grow,
Or bring down snow,
With her crippling blow.

She can uproot tree's,
With her forceful winds,
With a path of destruction,
Leveling everything within.

So when it comes to nature,
Remember who is in control,
She can tear us to pieces,
Or she can leave us whole.

Brian Allen Henry

TIME TO REFLECT

Sitting on my front porch,
Watching the world go by,
Surrounded by pines,
Looking back at younger times.

Alone with my thoughts,
Now I spend my days,
Reflecting on the past,
Where only dreams can stay.

Remembering the good times,
On this quiet overcast day,
I'm thankful for the moments,
That through the years have stayed.

The best years come and gone,
But my twilight lingers on,
Like an old song inside me,
For these days I long.

FEELINGS

Have you ever,
Been caught up,
In a moment,
Of anger?

Where true feelings,
Come to view,
You let loose,
What's true.

Then you regret,
What you said,
Words flow easy,
When misled.

So think awhile,
Before you explode,
Count to ten,
Ease the load.

Brian Allen Henry

PEACE OF MIND

Riding through the mountains,
On an old dusty trail,
A man and his horse,
His best pal.

They ride through silence,
Not a soul in sight,
Such a serene feeling,
All is right.

They stop by a stream,
To rest for a while,
Water for his pal,
Under the blue sky.

He sits on a rock,
Staring at the valley below,
A hawk soars above,
As time slows.

On this mountain trail,
His soul is at home,
He takes it all in,
Free to roam.

SEASIDE HOLIDAY

The sound of the seaside,
Tucked away in my mind,
When I was a young boy,
Visions lost in time.

I can smell the ocean,
It seems so real,
Gathering seashells in the sand,
Until my bucket was filled.

Building castles out of sand,
Such a grand day,
As I was a sculptor,
In my own way.

My mother and father,
Now gone from view,
Left me with memories,
And love so true.

Brian Allen Henry

MY OLD CREW

The old neighborhood,
Will never be the same,
Now that everyone,
Has moved away.

As I drive down,
The old avenue today,
Everything seems smaller,
Since I've been away.

I still hear the voices,
From the distant past,
Four boys laughing,
If only it could last.

Now we've all aged,
And moved on down the line,
But I'll never forget,
All the good times.

Hanging out with friends,
In days gone by,
Seeing their images,
Brings tears to my eyes.

DON'T GET IT

This electronic world,
Is getting me down,
It's filling my head,
With things I don't understand.

Log on log out,
It sounds like a jumble,
What's it all about,
Ask old Bill he's,
The wizard renown.

Text this, email that,
Send me a fax.
It makes me want,
To shout, I just,
Can't sort out,
What it's all about.

This old brain,
Wasn't programmed this way,
It's just a completely,
New world that leaves,
Me in a daze.

Brian Allen Henry

RAINY DAYS

Dark clouds move in,
There's a silence all around,
A strange eerie feeling,
As lightening touches down.

The heaven's open up,
As the rain hits the ground,
Soaking mother Earth,
With force abound.

People run for cover,
If there's any to be found,
The rain slowly softens,
As clouds move around.

The sun comes out,
There's freshness in the air.
The calm before the storm,
The danger's always there.

LOVE

Caring is sharing,
Sharing is love,
Love is something,
We never get tired of.

So when you see,
Someone in need,
Show them love,
Humanity's seed.

If they're hungry,
Give them bread,
If they're tired,
Give them a bed.

If there sick,
Get them care,
Love is the one thing,
We can all share.

16721033R00043

Made in the USA
Charleston, SC
07 January 2013